Rain Scald

MARY BURRITT CHRISTIANSEN POETRY SERIES
Hilda Raz, Series Editor

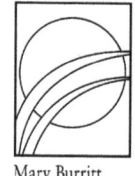

Mary Burritt
Christiansen
Poetry Series

The Mary Burritt Christiansen Poetry Series publishes two to four books a year that engage and give voice to the realities of living, working, and experiencing the West and the Border as places and as metaphors. The purpose of the series is to expand access to, and the audience for, quality poetry, both single volumes and anthologies, that can be used for general reading as well as in classrooms.

Also available in the Mary Burritt Christiansen Poetry Series:

For additional titles in the Mary Burritt Christiansen Poetry Series, please visit unmpress.com.

RAIN SCALD

Poems

Tacey M. Atsitty

University of New Mexico Press ~ Albuquerque

Library of Congress Cataloging-in-Publication Data
Names: Atsitty, Tacey M., 1982– author.
Title: Rain Scald: Poems / Tacey M. Atsitty.
Description: First edition. | Albuquerque: University of New Mexico Press, 2018. |
    Includes bibliographical references.
Identifiers: LCCN 2017005985 (print) | LCCN 2017021786 (e-book) |
    ISBN 9780826358677 (softcover : acid-free paper) | ISBN 9780826358684 (e-book)
Classification: LCC PS3601.T75 A6 2018 (e-book) | LCC PS3601.T75 (print) |
    DDC 811/.6—dc23
LC record available at https://lccn.loc.gov/2017005985

The author is grateful to the following journals for previously publishing some of the
    poems found in this book:
American Indian Culture and Research Journal: "Achi'íí'," "His Women," "Plum-to-Plum"
    (published as "Daddy's Women"), "Playground Notes," and "Stem Water"
As/Us Journal: "Dilute," "Paper Water," and "Sons of Carlisle"
bosque (the magazine): "On Receiving Revelation"
Crab Orchard Review: "At Evil Canyon" and "Razed"
Drunken Boat: "Bone Spur," "Downpour," "Flint Boys, Sky Map," and "Rain Scald"
Florida Review: "Calico Prints," "Mothway," and "S. Influenza—In Code"
Kenyon Review Online: "Vail Her Stallion"
Mandala Journal: "Elegy for Yucca Fruit Woman," "Monster Who Kicks People Down
    the Cliff," and "Rising Song, Elegy"
New Orleans Review: "At the Rim of Thought," "Awakening Song," "Evensong,"
    "Nightsong," "Recurrent," "Snake White, Owl White," and "To Gorge"
New Poets of the American West Anthology: "Calico Prints"
Perspectives: "Chokecherry Canyon," "Flight Bridge," and "Leaping Ridge"
Red Ink Magazine: "Anasazi," "In Dishwater," and "In Strips"
Talking Stick: Native Arts Quarterly: "Burial Waves" and "Salt Lick"
Yellow Medicine Review: "Alternate Sunrise"

Cover illustration: *Water Memory*, © Cara Romero, 2015
Designed by Lila Sanchez
Composed in Dante MT Std 11.5/13.5

*To my mother and sister
and others who no longer know
the feel of rain.*

Contents

Tóhee'

TSÉYI' Deep in the Rock

Snake White, Owl White

When I say my cheek fell,
I mean bone, gliding

pell, sunken. I mean it hides
in rain, in a sky-lit cell, swelling.

This is me fallen together,
separated from her: a mistelling

of Female Warrior Who Split
in Two, who pulled from her gut-well

a lumpy snake, pale with a scaling tongue.
Word-slit. I've heaved her pang, her yell

at the snap of his tail. They drop
into words at the end, a quell

to the flood line of a uvula,
face, cheek pouch—high shell

veins. Birds swim silver
in sky. An owl drops to dwell

with me. Gapes. *It's death.*
I step back. I can't tell

how he rises and dives at me, then turns
flight just before my head. When I tell you,

this is where bone rises to white,
I mean tomorrow, a minute later, dive well.

Ach'íí'

I
In my pocket: intestines
wrap fat, and it's so stiff
when cold. It looks like—

we shouldn't speak,
so young. Instead, knead salt,
flour, and water.

Our toys, I've tasted them:
sheepherders or soldiers.
Should they harden

and be painted, or should
a hole be blown from the insides.
All that salt.

II

Dad's baby brother, his intestines

broke, and he couldn't pee.

He died because he was so full.

Just like his grandmother,

the day she walked out of the hogan,

dropped to her knees, holding her

stomach—so mixed up inside

when it exploded.

III

After all those explosions in Vietnam, it must've messed my uncle up pretty good. He could never eat ach'íí' again. He had to have three Enemy Ways done. We had to haul so many sheep. It's a long ride in the back of a jeep all the way to Farmington to be baptized. I stood next to that wall of bricks at the Apache building, wearing my squash blossom: a line of females v'ing down to the male, and there rested his tongue, almost between my breasts.

IV

I remember She Who Wasn't Spoken Of—
each Red Vine costed a nickel, that easy twine

across the street from our little red-bricked
house—They say she drove so fast

she whorled into a puff of smoke
behind Table Mesa the day she died.

Dad says he remembers the first time he died,
that long bus ride when they took him

to Utah for school. He had been memorizing
land formations: an angel the size of his hand

disappeared, and after that he was so empty
from crying and so full of remembering

rocks, he just fell asleep. He remembers
stealing pennies from his foster sister

to buy red licorice. He was always in trouble
for that or for sling-shotting chickens.

Only three survived the morning massacre.
Only one sheep was taken from the flock.

They stole it, all those Navajo boys,
led it to the mountain edge, where
they built a fire and slit its throat:

laughing into the dry
night, fat dripping
from their mouths.

Sunbeam

Around noontime on Highway 666, we are driving to town. It is Pepper's fifth birthday. My dad is working. He is probably running laps with students. *Cloudless.* Our two vehicles leave the Chuskas. I want a sucker. Cheii takes me south. There are six of them in the other car; they turn north. It is too bright today. Two weeks ago my mom dreamt of night birds chanting amid juniper berries. Today, the land formations look like owls. I leave Little Water Trading Post with Minnie Mouse's heart in my mouth. Pepper is singing, "Jesus Wants Me for a Sunbeam," with our cousin-sister when—Mom was holding Baby in the front passenger seat and shot a look over to her sister—My little brother sips root beer while Baby sleeps. It was May. I sit alone in the back of my cheii's truck, wiping rouge across my eyelids. I don't understand the dream or the land—Grandma clenches my hand as we stand on the road, watching the sun take them:

peppergrass gathered in a pink cup, here, Daddy.

Rising Song, Elegy

To Pepper

I

Shádí, immersed in canyon,
it was so wet that spring,

this summer. We gripped
our Easter sacks: a time of

knowing. You knew when I was
about to—Rain, see how it eats
the mouths of our paper sacks,

how it drowns hollow tree
sounds we'd make when leaving
each other in the early dark.

II

In a photo of us, you were purple,
and I stood in a flower: desert bloom.
Your eyes cradled me. Now, I feel only
your wilt. My cheeks say you must've
meant vine and petal to me.

III

A whistle
    tore out of my throat—

IV

Give in to you, falling:
in breath, we begin to waft.

It's about to rain at the curve
of mine. I feel all wrought

when I see stars we never sang
through: so many girls in scatter—

Calico Prints

It was morning when she left, her pockets filled with bones. A small stack of round flatbread steamed beneath cloth. After she stoked the fire, she stepped toward the hogan exit. At the sides of aspen, she staggered northeast, barefoot, toward the tree line. Her hands dripped yucca-root foam. One hand gripped her stomach, the other reached to where the mountain flats break the blue contour. She was on her knees when it exploded, her skirt muddied. Her clay fingers held ghost beads. It was the water she drank, soaked in tailings. Many nights she had lain in sheepskin, damped. That morning the firmament unraveled into a bolt of aqua calico. She stepped into yards of apricot blooms, carried herself in her skirt, steps and steps. *Stemless blossoms.* She followed patterns of earth and saw how they matched the floral sky:

her children tracked staggered footprints to the wash's edge.

Elegy for Yucca Fruit Woman

"Without me," she said. Go—
I'm going to the rock
that once had wings. My life
rolls like rock clods
down a volcanic throat, circling
the tips of big winds beneath

~

poised arms   *wing bone, surrounded*
and closing, dust hinge. In upstroke, a slow
separate   in landing then takeoff. To take
air, those inward whooshes   as if blessing
oneself: marrow leaving the hollow

~

pop. She knelt with women
filling the earth: mush in tin
after tin, filled in with breaking
sun. Kneeling down, she'd flap
dough with the wood pop,
her hands whirring. The air
bubbles rising with heat ready to—
Later she'd send me to 7-2-11
clenching quarters for—

~

At two points: they say a man flew
with a life-feather, quill in hand,
from the top of Shiprock down
to the people, having slain
monster birds. Plumes
and all their vanes ending
in flight after bird strike.

~

"A female eagle swooped east,"
she once told me. "It was like gold
whirring in the blue of my wind-
shield. I was in my truck, driving
and listening to peyote songs
when it happened. I had never seen
so much dust."

~

When skin slats, layered
like stone, then collapses—

a red grows gray. Aspen expands
to the hush

of this cedar-filled room. When
her neck grew heavy she said,

"The music helps me; press play."

Hei hei ya wena hei nei, Hei hei ya wena hei nei;
Hei hei ya wena hei nei, nei; Hei hei ya wena hei nei;
Ya na hei ya na hei o weno hei nei;
Ya na hei ya na hei o weno hwoi na hei nei yo wei.

Vail Her Stallion

When shoes no longer lace the pond line,
we stamp leaves to cover or push summer

where rain scarcely pools to wrap children.
Homemade ice cream melted on my tongue

the other night as I choked on the menthol.
"Stay away from there; the Brownhat girl, she drowned

in there," my uncle told me. "A stallion, too." Weeds
wound with wave and current; they wrapped her ankles

in a deep tunnel of—just kept her berserk
in the hole where she was found bobbing, caught up,

clouds drifting from her eyes. Stallion, all black shine:
he must've shone like water as wind veiled him, mane

and all. I imagine the hole like mint ice cream
or milkweed when it beads out at the throat.

In the mountains, I gathered mint to boil for jars of jelly.
I gifted one to each family member. "Is this from—"

they would ask, and upon twisting off
the lid, they'd close it tight. The sharpness

cracked their lips, as they recalled her mane
gone trepid in the tug and snap of vines.

Playground at Sunset

Prologue

Go without water on days like these, mouth
dry as sagebrush, know to blow on shallow
pools of rainwater before drinking.
Point to where a woman pulls water
out of a rock, but a young child knows not
to ask for what is not in front of her.

I

I thought it was a treat to be left
for hours, to seesaw the day
away, to run through tires
erected in dirt and to sit inside
them when wind or rain came.

I'd imagine sitting inside with Joey.
They say he kissed Heather in there.
Once he touched the burn on my forehead:
"Ouch. That must've hurt." Never had a boy
touched me so tenderly. Then we ran
to the swings and he gave me an underdog.

II

Inside the tire, in its darkness we wait.
Only my little sister is young enough to utter,

"When's Daddy coming back?" When howl
and rain are done, we walk to the edge

of the playground to write our names
in the sandbox then smooth them out.

III

Can I just say I got tired of waiting,
that it got too hard—the solidified salt
tear from inside.
                    Someone knife-scratched
I love Tacy into the back of a door,
so the teacher shut me in a room
during recess because she thought
I carved my love for myself.

IV

Even with my brother and sister's weight combined,

it wasn't enough—
                        to teeter-totter me into the air,
but that didn't matter.
                    They were in sky,

yee-hawing in clouds.

V

This isn't the first   time I've lain
beneath bars: horizontal   ladder
or bed   spring, with the wind

knocked out,   hard-packed dirt
and gravel or tile at my back.

In this position   I take
sky's weight, feel his hand. When   unable

to move or whimper,   lie—
plead thin   clouds to drop

and fill me with breath,
to iron out the   stuttered heaving.

VI

I learned not to answer my little sister
until sunset calmed our skin, ready
for a deep bruise to fill the night.

"Soon."

His Women

I
She looked like me, but she wasn't
my mother. She took me to the store
without him; this woman bought me
a locker bag. I zipped secrets in there,
where it smelled like candy. Her first gift
to me was pink lip balm; I never used it.
When she left, I asked him why.
"Because she likes me," he answered.

II
I knew the word *sex*; it was private.
On TV, I'd seen long-haired men

point their guitars up and wail, "She's my cherry
pie." One morning I found a cherry pie lying

hog-tied on the floor, asleep in her own urine.
I knew he had been a bull rider

but hadn't known about him calf-roping.
I circled around her into his room.

"That's Belle," he answered. "Go fix breakfast
while she sobers up." I stepped over her

and stood at the stove—pushing fat around—
waiting for that salty smell to drown the house.

Plum-to-Plum

He was a gift giver, the kind who'd buy in bulk from the flea market. He'd keep them high up in a kitchen cabinet for times such as this: sometimes they were turquoise earrings, sometimes bronze bangles or packets of stickers. Tonight it was a Precious Moments pocket calendar. He probably decided on this gift so he could forget today, or maybe so I could remember, or perhaps to link these days together like vines looping plum-to-plum on our kitchen wall. To me, they always looked like bruised fruit splotched across a woman's body—tonight I study the egg-headed blonde on the pocket calendar, her forced smile. Already I am crying, but I cry harder for her and her smile and eyes. Eyes hang on her face like raindrops ready to drip her story. Then I realize she knows what I've known all these years. And she was sad for me, sad how I'd gone about forgiving, how I'd bury these gifts in the backyard, and how when he'd pull me near, I'd stand stiff as a moon in February, blank faced and without any regard for his arms wrapped around me.

In Dishwater

In my childhood kitchen I'd have to boil
dishwater, one kettle, maybe two. I was still
a child when I wrinkled into the old woman
I am now. When water rose past my shoulders,
scars from my legs to my scalp arose in my hands.
Only then did they become visible to me—Our kettle
didn't scream or howl; it just steamed quietly. Sometimes
I'd forget about it until water let go into air, or until it hissed
over flame. Then I'd come running. In my childhood kitchen,
one wipe smeared a girl across countertops, smeared her
hair gray like old dishwater. There was only the appearance
of neat—In the calm clink of silverware, I'd try to recall
the first time I slammed a cabinet or drawer shut, wonder
when my loathing of silverware began. How long had my hands
been scalded in dishwater, grabbing for knives or forks.

Alternate Sunrise

After Diane Reyna's Abiding Force #3, *2002*

slanted strip of black, a finger traces
in the ginger pool
   bows a menstrual-streaked border

cold side of this wall
   breath whips, voices—the pane

flurries meander adobe
   like mourning dove's tune

when clouds rotate: elevated zigzag

   water off cardboard, rushes
beneath trash, holds clothes
   red tie oscillates from fingers

to eye, bloodshot in morning

   see a scratched list, still tilted
into crimson Pendletons; wrong temperature

   bamboo rests on a glass mouth, shoots intertwined
a sprout almost reaches
   the ripple of green water

Stem Water

I

We offer icicles to our father on newspaper.
We allow fire to follow us. We clink until altogether
we break—my brother and I kneel outside
in snowfall at sundown. It set as we lit kindling.
Out here, I handle ice like the skeletal frame of a fan,
hold them between flame and me, closer until closed.
Icicles appear as bone. When fire reaches through
our fingers, I realize the half-life of an ice stick—

II

Dad says it smells like a funeral. His bride wilted
with her bouquet in a separate way. It hangs
upside down in the mudroom, the bouquet
kept in a still January hold. A flower arrangement
passes on, passes through tubes of lilies rising.

I think to throw them out—unblossomed as they are—
or put them to rest above the kitchen sink, or offer them
to loved ones, so their stench no longer culls visions
of matured blooms in a basket, no longer clouds
or salts stem water.

III

I should be eating protein right about now.
I read once in a poem that no one should eat
this much cake, but here I am at five a.m. losing
my tongue to tiers of butter and salt. After four
thick slices, I can taste it all—every ingredient.
I've learned cascading is much like gorging,
that sugar is not really so sweet as it is salty.
After I burned my tongue on granule
after granule, it's nothing new, almost familiar:
such a thick, swallow frost.

Salt Lick

I left myself,
a heifer to her salt block, to carve hip bone.
Coxal deposits tinge dry. In the nape's shelf,
a jar of salt: I lost myself in granules; prone
now to live life with a chiseled tongue, worn
rare to the tip. It feels like that, like everything
needs salt. Even lipoma tastes better adorned
at the mouth of a gorge, in thick chrysalis bling.
I folded myself calmly. Hands in V: rush
and ready to dive, just a sleek dip into beef stock,
for a moment, a pastoral hush—
This is me mooing. Death comes heavy: pock
marks squirm ringworm. Ribeye. See the pooling
grease, what's left of me: ribbon of fat, how it spools.

When Water Came to Me

For a moment, all that once ribbed between us fell still.
In a moment, all that once ripped within us falls still.
So I thrust my thighs forward, curls to break our still.

These aren't natural occurrences for me, he said.
This is how nature occurs in me, I said.
We had enough drip between us to run off and shed—

I thought to weigh in, to starve myself off in ~
I thought to wade in, to stave myself off with ~
But when my hair is down, I stand as a horse in ~

I thought I had learned to wade without waiting.
Yes, I thought I had learned to wait without wading.
When my legs are wet up to here, I come close to fading

in—water: it's so oblivious; it eats through my coat hair,
eats through my coat hair and leaves me winterbare.

GORGE DWELLER

Rain Scald

When standing (in rain) for so long, you no longer hear
or feel it falling—you believe it's stopped. Step away—

look to your (skin; muck itch. It's a) shame, your hands
have gone bald from fungus. Taking you to (what's beneath scab,

to) one of those nights when you know (your gums will bleed.
To say) it's been a while or it has to do with (wrist mange

is to say rot comes so easily now, skin weep—) lapse. Step through
the whole (black of your home) and still know damp, know

(exactly when to bend your finger for) the light switch.

ˋ   ˋ   ˋ

so familiar (in aubade)

shame, your hands

have gone haywire. Taking you to (what's beneath rust: ranges

they've grazed—) a time

when you're combed through

when you know your knuckles—

and all that rain has swallowed.

Recurrent

For Reuben

A hairpipe choker hangs across the gorge:
bone beads fastened at the neck, fallen ladder
down his back, into the humble. Stones
sit heavy in his rucksack, name tape ripped:
his name frays black like the whorls
of his fingertips. Long days he'd sit
on boards, knotted like waves, kneading
out knots with the mountains of his knuckles.

At Cloud Dance, we learned origin follows
prayer song. He's seen origin settle like fog
into eyes as fists reach for the dark. *Cloud-pull
is dust storm and desert is battle pool.* Out of
the word-water a letter drops from his name: E
leaves Reuben windburned. Soldier Boy held
up by coils in ribbon: him in his Class A's,
all decorated in purple, in rib. At his side, a child
etches an E into the gorge floor.

The child asks about true knots, about a witch
who stitches skin of children to make her bag.
"If she finds me down here, in these thought
puddles, am I inviting her to come? And her hands,
are they as coarse as the rope about your neck,
Soldier Boy?"

       Before it scabs, he holds it
with a cold rag, steeps his neck in ice water
until pain stops. But in the billow of night, enemies'
faces pull, eyelets cloud. Was he that numbing
I was to watch for? *Songs about the cheeks of fire.*
I dreamt him wading in a whirl near Warm Springs:
at the eye a lone hill, a black hill—gone to tug
at his hair, now an aerial blur.

Recurrent soldier suspended in sky. *A running knot,*
a straight slip. Last Thursday, slack. Looses his pony tail
and collapses like silk, blacks into the drain.

Burial Waves

I
They say they look blue from afar,
but up close they're green and gleam
like scales of sirens. Tongues invite: *come
inside*. It's usually birds who end up telling.
Their quick flight from the rocking, plumes
left in haste. Pasted to the big wave sky.
The animals, they know. Know always before—
they feel for the coming. Along the steps,
Coyote scurries in a robe, a bulge at his side.
She's rushing for her babies (Water Monster)
and the wall precedes her coming. Waves
clip the fins of fish, leaving behind nothing
but spine and ribs.

II

He went somewhere smoke
cannot bless, stepped down
the stone staircase where waves
now swell over, leaving
a line of caulk along the steps.
He's sucked in where waves lap
gorge walls. Where he went,
water gives way to no body.
Where he's stuck: ledges rise
beneath, carved. Overhanging
he tumbles into white pockets.
A soft churn: boiling, boiling.
When he's stuck in undercurrent,
in crevice, come in ash and only—
smeared. Skin invisible and without
water, making his way to the unsleeping still.

Nightsong

To the gorge dwellers

With no fire, you offer
nothing. Say,

a body found, fall creek
gorge. Eventual

it is, meaning to happen.
Meaning to say,

Dear fellow _____,
It is with deep

Name—Name—
Name, strung like

hair. Water strands
made old, made

white. Too close
to dark. Second tragedy

fall creek throat.
Repeated repeated loss.

Thirst-in almanac
of the gorges. Litany

of wrists. Look
down at your wrists,

down here where
the thick laps

the lips. Where you
haven't been taught:

pull yourself out of
the plunge pool

and look for fire, look
for rings shifted

to your thumb and
forefinger. There, like

vapor wrapping you
in strips. In this falling

moment, cities
sink into the depths,

drown. The earth
face carried up and

away in the current of
a whirlwind, where water

and mountains hide
in deep blue. What faces

bring: a reservoir filled,
following the night

when day fell into day,
soon followed by night

into night to night,
thrice with no moon,

thrice with no flame—
kept in the thick thick.

At the Rim of Thought

> When I stand here, I want to jump into the canyon. It's a psychological
> desire to want to become one with what's more powerful than us.
>
> —*Tséyi'*, Laura Tohe

To sleep off this cliff
when sky pushes me heavy—
wood:stone as cradleboard:canyon.
To close my eyes, my lips.

In a room full of wives and ones to be, I cradle
a son in board, walk him fingers in palms.

In this arch: is it really so bad *hanging*
clouds would they even care *land swallow* will they say
she's so stupid for *crevice slit* where did she get them
anyway *mud pebbles* and for how long did she hold
them *stone inlay* in palm before chasing them

down the gorge of her throat. When someone utters
leap, it doesn't always mean *snap*. From ridge
follow that waterfall: so afraid to retreat in step before

taking the north flight; it's the only way. Without note—
it's all without. To sleep these knots loose. The steaks
will be ready in an hour. Is it enough flesh
to make anyone care? Conversations hooked in arm,
silent. A nest the size of a palm, tilted and bare
in winter hedge. See cassette ribbon tape: musicality,
junk, and nature. The care gone into the weave,
spirals bark-thin and waves so small, soft for the coming—

gone—those who hatched. They are flying now,
gathering thread for new nests. If I had a daughter,
she'd be curling her hair now. Now in rollers,
cooling. How long did she hold them *straight unravel*
beneath her beak: bird eggs or pale blue seeds.

Just one. Of all of these—salt-fisted. She counts *that silent walk.*
She utters cold beneath the still and leaves earplugs
on the sill. In an hour, she will carve the steak *an unfastening*
of sand lips birth like death from the same tree.

She will pull herself from blankets, creased
over fallen walls, and though—she'll still be—tired
she knows she will have slept.

Flight Bridge

Carnation ruffle:

red web swell.

One white rose

(mist) left, laid

to calm on

concrete, right

into the curve

of bars. See—

they embrace,

so much to say.

See pipe cleaners

weave into wings

linking the hours.

Bone Spur

I told myself, "Bááhadzid." It means I told my hand
to be careful because it looked harmless.

Mine were palms once bruised. Now they lift
like snowflakes, a flit and sunder at even haaaa.

It's not that I don't want loose. Ice worms
recumbent from wriggle expand, and my wrist
bone goes swollen with freeze.

I lament how wrist joins forearm to hand.
                    palms turn like face

Thin tubes of empty, I lip
a sucking song, one that melts
the ice beads from my joints.

But I can no longer abide singing male parts
in addition to female vocables. I am breathless
by the time I begin my own.

That is to say, I don't invoke water.
I am most agreeable in drought,
but fear the far tingle and burn of hands.

The problem is my love abides only in ice storm.

The truth is my wrists lock even at the waft of flame,
at the grain of hair rubbing together in a hand towel,
at the smallest drizzle on my palms.

Awakening Song

Entire orchard taste: a small ways off
from mouth foam. He'll scoff,

she doesn't know sweet like this, can't gnaw
on fruit like this: such a flesh whisper, raw

innards to skin peel. Rife with seed.
Apron string like stem, ripe weed

twirl, slope down the core: black side
and in. Chafe. Lips bruise, abide

about the neck like rubies, so fresh
& swollen. Who could have such a flesh

appetite? The crunch and chew
that follow drool from origin of ew.

When she cuts a Red Delicious horizon-
tally, the star core gazes, waxing her fun.

Squeeze. Pome so plump with sweat—
taste unwritten. Lip bruise treat

lingers long past sugar blossom. Buds
of her tongue know granule like studs

know the ear. They're pointing at her:
head and heel. A whistle ache from her

throat. The dry follows briars ground
to powder. Wipe it across the sound

of her voice. She doesn't yield to seed-set
diamonds in his mouth. Shimmery wet

scales, a reflection of windows from roof
collapse. There is pollen on her chin. Poof!

With one huff, she labors to her knees,
leaving the belly trail of pleas—

In her calm, she tore into sands of the sea,
craving salt from a different flesh.

To Gorge

After Separation of the Sexes, Diné Creation Story

She steps into the powder magazine, bustle
in hand. Left to sediment, spur mud chips
in a cloud of musk. *Linger.* Left to hustle
with stripped cacti: rub into the hips
of a woman, this side of the river—
      O wretched hussy!
What is not forsaken? These lips
about a warmed cask. *Lap.* There is nothing
beautiful about gorging, not a thing:
dregs lazing down the barrel—
      O wretched grease!
Left to thicken into smoke: she can
do that all by herself, tallow queen
spread across the rise and curl of every squeeze.
      Wretched be the appetite and creosote of man!
She explodes without them, sulfur and honey.

Downpour

I asked him down here:

where virgin belts dangle from my thighs

where my sash belt pulls the sky in, knuckles go white, and all
without a moan

where leaves turn so quickly, already red with winter

where we wait for deluge, but it never comes

not yet ripe, only vocables can embody

Down here, I can't pull out of this tune to utter

the cowardice of hand and tongue   what I wanted

I can't tear myself from this heap of blankets; this rocking comfort, my—

self: the only one I allow

and our son, I leave him, like a monster, cooing in the next gorge over

/

I can't sing over the onrush of falling water, that pounding connect from
mouth to base

lick cloudburst, the way I want

Down here, I speak with a tongue of cedar: bark and kindle

the clouds last night, they held back

But like I said, we shouldn't chant what's not ours

he sacks himself up for me to unravel

a bag of pears. I give one to him, and it gushes with each pull of skin

/

And still I can't tear away from these blankets

even when he says he's ready for downpour:

I offer him my hand to guide me down the gorge

But don't play my flute for him; I don't want him to fall in—

with me, like I did. I strum him so thinly, and still he chants

I am left to cramp, my entire body over

/

I bring him down here to let my hair loose, then ask him to put it in a knot

my confidence is worn to warps, a bald fringe

my breath no longer shapes syllables of his name

he says rain and I go beautifully together

what it means to apologize

how I curl my hair even though my wrists ache for him

how my nails chip before the moons push on through

how I cross my legs for him as he blows at rain

his fingers wrap our silence

how I prefer the heavens to rainfall

how for him, I am all of this—as sorry as I am when I say,

The sky is so hollow from child.

Marked

We ripple into sediment, they   wrote,
as though we are grays   staggering
the river bottom; milky hard and   thrown
about, not stained pebbles pieced   together
in the form of beats, curved and   edged
by strikes. Our light catches even in   shards,
from gravel. A channel sparks   face
and heart: they think charred   skin
and charcoal don't shine. For a   time
ignited with wool tinder, this all   leaves
a deep hue isolated. It's just now   sunrise
and silt sinks flint that once took the   shape
of a heart. Here we lie like pores of an   arrow-
head, awaiting the day when stone turns to   water.

On Receiving Revelation

> Man must be governed by an understanding of his natural surroundings.
> The earth is under the protection of something which at times becomes
> visible to the eye.
>
> —Teton Sioux Medicine Man

The pines are webbed heavy with winter,
In times of white over green, wise over enough—
Erase talc lines with a wet rag, a smeared flow
of voices. Know what is visible, what rise
comes from the lull of snow, what cusp
of uncertainty follows. Meander ice

trails wound in season like a drum's lacing. Ice
in hand, smear these slats clear from winter
or all things old. Is it not enough to sing the cusp
closed? So empty with song, so resonant of an eye
fluttering at the push of flakes. All that rises
must someday slip. Somewhere beneath shells flow

this and many other pleas. Ask for the taut flow
of visibility, for more than the *to get through* ice,
to work through, to overcome all things ice, to rise
through horsetails and fans of cascade winters.
Turn to kneel at the gorge steeple, and wait for eyes
to wane with snow cut's stratum, in deluge, in cusp.

What is visible to eye clasp, eye cusp
crusted with rime. In palms glazed seeds flow.
What grips the ground of unseen. Marble eye,
through whiteout, sees glass glimmer. Ice
sugar, quiver of bolts: both lightening and ray. Winter
in sand closing, fractured. In truth: fall, rise,

fall again into straps of gorges. Here, rise
among women, pose lines to curve the cusp,
pose a bottle of pills returned, pose a pile of winter
unleavened. Take them from me because flow

comes with the taking. Blessing of thaw and drip: ice
cackle no more to stiffen nor whip the eye.

An answer drifts in sky board; my eyes
glint in certainty at the snow line. As water rises,
pull out from plunge, chips of ice
chalk melt into an overflow of light. Cusp
in the falling: awake with cherubim. Flow
atop the pines. Look! Walls loll in sun's winter:

in cycles of ice, in circles of the eye;
spring will winter, and God's sorrow rises
to the cusps of his eyes: a swivel of fire flow.

TÓHEE'   Extinct Navajo ceremony
used for calling rain, healing paralysis,
resuscitating from drowning and deafness,
and handling dreams

In Strips

I

fingertip knead
this rickrack struggle
in the spread
crosswire threads
muscle like crevice
nose of mountain

neck, stitch issue
line by blossom
wrap, sat on
warp-and-weft effect
bless, us up-stitch
collar, yeah

sentence tear
rest on fault
my wrist, the roundup
when we gather
song, yeah
or ugly

II

bark, take care
or or or
or wrinkle
or smear nickels
settle into letters
word at the bottom
zhiins, over the i

language we use
beyond that
rub flower
into clavicle
clip them
these are elbows
like stars, skin

push it around
gather the hip
or compass
pick moments—
break rickrack
says, either page
quilt, look up

III

let me respond, stick
private as armpit
where the skin
of land keeps
know there's infant
lava rock is not lava
leap in all
forehead, nose

out our ribs:
I am sorry, say
gathers, let me
in our strife
within the rocks
rock, but blood—
fury, from ridge
chin to breasts

tiering course
that again, sip
swing, storytell
pass by pass
within the guts
know of monsters
to fall, water trace
tummy to knees

IV

but this, this
stress on the fold
bark of wrinkle
and piecing
hills to sky, land
like mountain sack

is not a mountain
is not a gorge, align
what binds the raw
of built up or collapse
altogether, words
gone with the grain

is seam rip seam
is walls in back stitch
edge, the sashing
of create, appliqué
like clouds, sentence
in strides of bark

At Evil Canyon

Where I'm going there is no water:
where rain thins into streaks of hair,

beneath bangs, at the right cheek,
looking at me bowl faced. Like molars

tucked in the back of a mouth.
Four masks in a row, marked bare

by posts, sun-blanked board, fallen.
A woman comes to me, "Do they sing?

How did this wall tilt? Which infant
pushed off, stomped the cracks

of this face?" Hand-hand and hand-hand
tell me a saliva sojourn, all along the wall.

Bow my head to light, heat reflect.
Here shark head emerges from canyon

waves; scale them. And with finger
shadows pluck ants from the ground.

"If you've never seen them, you'll never see
them (faces nor hands)," she said. "As a girl

I searched these walls but never found them.
Here, where rocks rise like gnarled fingers."

To know your hands is to dip them
into lake clouds, a rock-deep cool.

Leaping Ridge

The Crescent tells of a night that once poured
pale tiles out of the sky. A pail tilt—
whoosh! Night blooms from Spanish Dagger, sores
of water in ash. There is no smoke spilt
or stitches along fibers: land to blue.
Wall where water carves a tear, a wilted
pluck or flower canal. Gourd-full spew
at the tongue. Watch how a sheer quilt
freezes in patch, in dune. *Smother.* Rock-
fold once cradled a mother in the hilt,
dipped her in descent. *Yucca curl.* Last gawk
went in search of her back, where after the jolt,
her infant swayed: at every crumble of limb and mud,
such a small thud, thud, thud.

Monster Who Kicks People Down the Cliff

He tells me his mother once rode a mare to death, that when he was a child, she'd kick him in the pants and he'd plummet to the canyon floor, talking to his relatives along the way. But tonight the sky emits a loneliness only a monster could know, and so he told me how he came to be this way. In a vale of cottonwoods, he starts. My mother would sit near a river, bending her back for stones that looked like half of me. Soon thereafter, I settled like a rock inside her belly as she rode bareback along the river. Maybe it was the weight of me, but soon she regretted how she waited for the sun to warm cliffs, regretted my father seeing her longing—I've seen her clamber and wail when she went off to be with canyon walls! Later, she'd rock me to sleep: *O wei o na o wei o naa, o wei o na o wei o na'oho, o wei o nei o naa o wei o wei naa.* And as she went riding over, I can't tell you how the sky shot me to pieces. How my insides lay like a wet mane over river rocks. I never saw the horse again. And now, my mother's people know nothing but to skid me across water into the walls below. Your people, he finishes and stands up:

When you pile the night as long as I have,
and wait for walls to sink then rise into sun,
you can never know morning like this—

Chokecherry Canyon

It's more than fruit itself. Rot:
long past the budding. Bitter skin,
we are taught to spit it out, all wrought
on the ground, foaming. Men,
in their haze, breathe in Black Cats
and take scars like stomachs of women.
A flesh so acidic, so hollowed bats
rarely cave there. Where hands of men
rock skulls to rock. Like chokecherries
leaving parched trails in your mouth,
so hard to swallow. Dik'ǫ́ǫ́zh: tongue carries
a shrivel to the throat and pulls eyelids south.
A bluster from the dry neck steeple:
O the depravity of my people!

Anasazi

How can we die when we're already
prone to leaving the table midmeal
like Ancient Ones gone to breathe
elsewhere. Salt sits still, but pepper's gone
rolled off in a rush. We've practiced dying
for a long time: when we skip dance or town,
when we chew. We've rounded out
like dining room walls in a canyon, eaten
through by wind—Sorry we rushed off;
the food wasn't ours. Sorry the grease sits
white on our plates, and the jam that didn't set—
use it as syrup to cover every theory of us.

Mothway

Push off the husk—glide the dusk-lit
sidewalk. Arms like wings, he bends
to appear shorter. Gray shorts, trailing scars
from ankle to thigh. It's that high: "Hurry and come,"
he says. Man, a vein collapse, a flutter at my face.
He turns tables, taps letters and curves in a rush

to a T. Graffiti: *I am the beast and end.* Rushing
along black sandpaper. A bolt wraps light
into soft white, wings cool in flap. He faces
falling skies, pushes powder on bulb's bend,
bids me come. But with burnt dust, I know *come*
invites only end's rising, because cars

do doughnuts in my chest, leaving skid-marked scars
along glass. *You are making me crazy.* Wanting to rush
into every fire. Come moth madness! Come!
seizure that twists and distorts, that follows
what is broken: his cheeks already—

A bird holds him by the face.

Rainboy stole his cousin's axe to crack the enemy's face
from neck up to skull—story of butterfly.
        To punish a scar-
red body: beam it up to coals as fire bends
death. Not aglow, not alight like butterfly, but rush
at it, letting it lick him brittle.
        —I dreamt him carted away in a cage of sticks. "Come

on," he said, then turned to pluck venom from his scales. "Come
on," he repeated. And I thought I saw a man on his knees, facing
a ceremony behind a chain link fence, on the corner graveyard
in Bernalillo: a boy on a bench, face scar-red.
He spoke with a puppet bird.

Always late, looks and rushes
but never goes. A sigh, a flutter of rampage, gliding the bend,

ending there at the bend. How ghastly his nostrils fall from his face!
He pants upside down then comes. He envisions fog of brown scars
after the rush, but oh, the clink of wire falling on white light.

S. Influenza—In Code

To the enemy listening,

A sheep   weasels   ice with a   needle into your   ear.

Your   skin itches, your   nose. A Ute catches a   flying insect while
  red ants pull   iron with a   needle from   elk.

It is in you:

a water snake   ices your   intestines with   tea. There is an   itch
on your   snout. Something   soapweed   oil from   mother's brother
cannot cure.

Like a ch'įįdii pressing an   awl into the   seeds of your   eye and
  ear. Etchings   match the sting of   yucca.   Weasel rubs moving
  stones, tearing at the tips.

> Grab from the sick pig box,
>
> Ross Haskie Sr.

Paper Water

After SB 2109

X threads us into rope, a weave of human
arms X'ed down a canyon wall. Voice

writes nights like these and calls
for complete night, without

scraps of light or dissonance or stuttered
cries. Crumble of tree limbs: X, there

we are again. This is how far we climb
for life. We'd rub out before reaching

the ground, where water cuts—
Once a man had only water to pray with.

Once life is the blur of a windmill,
each crisscross sets another arm

to bark. Cessation of the line; break
it up there. Article X: delineate marginal

arcs, say everything within windmill shot—
Whereas injury to water was writ

and concluded: how far inside earth
will they reach? Whereas for groundwater,

they steady their wrists for a slow up-stitch
across their own eyelids.

Sons of Carlisle

In circum, in house   turning
on wheels, dust of morning. Spin

to be the last—wallowing
in line. Because a snake splits,

leaves its hole. Because we no longer
part smoothly. A son altered

to crisp like diagonals of a snake
shedding. Do you see the marks?

Insignias of names whorl over,
quiet you. See a wrist roll widely

when completing a capitol O in air,
in name. When I speak my name

from behind the oculus, casualties
of letters, headstones can't cap words.

In our own words, mounds in rows: skills
to chisel, to sign one's name in stone

faces. The wave of a fescue, one son
with a lye tongue, spits bars, and lathers

new marks: Abraham, Edward, George,
Joseph, Isaac. These are they who were

once taught to look, to pray with eyes
open. Boys shed childhood names,

later they become men of their wives,
and stay sons to one—An altar of hair

half-bound, half-loosed, fraying, falls
at their feet. Final step is to brush off

like clouting   dust from the cuffs of pants
before stepping   into the house.

Dilute

After Rabbit Proof Fence

Wind to throw
an infant strapped
in cradle, to hide

and gallop away. Cut
off. Waving paper–
fanion of oxen

piss. The dead
animal so black,
says, "You go

to school to steal
children. Take me
to substance, to

fallen spine, nuggets
of bone." In waves
we were taught

with word, this paper
crinkle, wave ring white:
massacre of names.

Suck marrow, ink
curls in water. Mothers
heap, howl in sand—

step in rain, on stone.
Finally whisked to snow,
whirled away in letters.

Rain gives an edge. Look
for signs. They tell you
where to sit. Trace angels

smooth into one. Extend
your palm like this, it means:
You give me water.

Flint Boys, Sky Map

I

We memorize maps on a different back,
the back way. Uncrinkled paper skin,
like land of our knuckles. We know

how to get back, how hills stack
against morning moon. Crescent so thin,
tilted, the Flint Boys begin to row.

II

Ask them which way is up, or east,
their eyes wind the answer: a rain so female,
sun daggers dim in their pupils.
Mornings when ankle loads of scars

itch. The Holy People sprinkle a feast
over the monoliths. A male
rain so big they'd come to pull
upward from their legs, into the bars

III

of their heads. They step this warp
to know a great-grandmother,
a Hand Trembler, who knew land
and stars, taught them to memorize knots

of barbed wire: they were too new and sharp.
And this way his pain was boy. A father
cried in the moonlit bus, tracing the arches.
After hours, he rose with the glimmer dots.

Hand Trembler

hand   year-old

concentrate, what's lost

a loom, a Yellowhorse illness

people would

identify and remedy her lost   different patients

Hand trembler, I see her

trembling, tremble.   Ndeelniihii. Come

and talk. They wanted a way,

inside the hogan, the season

didn't matter. A sheep. Roll up

her right sleeve, eyes closed—

They come, almost always, they come

from the white. Find, given perspective

of a six. Her from everywhere, arm

exposed. Bring it up, that great-grandmother, hand extended.
Sees sideways,

turns her head, shaking

her

Razed

It's almost time for the day that falls
backward. We're done with ordinary mending
of enclosure. We came here wanting—coral
in the early morn. Originally, we came here to drop
like fallen posts and staples or nails—

Back before the wind spurred us haywire,
to the lone stump veering into jawbone,
when our hands tightened into rust, fingernails
chipped into shells, when moons mended
nothing. That's when I tore off and dropped
to where lambs squeeze out of the corral.

A baby hill, downtrodden like a forgotten corral
up north. Signs in picture form: Why are
boulders falling? Watch for limbs dropping
at the curves. Sharp ones, how at nightfall
wrists spur into corral. The mending
keeps lines taut. We look to salvage nails

fallen in dust. Posts with their teeth (bent nails)
are all that's left when a family leaves corrals.
All other wood is singed into sky. Mending
memories: I came with my father to pull at wire.
"This is where the hogan once stood." *Fallen
nails.* "And the opening of the corral—" He drops

the story from his mouth. His tongue drops
like coral chunks into a coffee can. Pebbles, nails
shaken with a wire handle: the sound falls,
making coyotes and bears go round: a choral
tumble of rocks lets them know: Here, I once was.
Here, I've searched for rust and metal, and mended

circles. I've taken to metal detectors, to mend
diamond rings, nails, and nickels; all dropped

by someone at some time. The ring settles to wire,
the axed tree dries, is gathered, stacked, and nailed.
Here, I've come to listen for the crunch of coral
beneath my boots or chants from dust. I fall

into mend, biting straight these nails,
hammer in hand, I drop in the corral—
All about me is wire, winding down like fall.

Evensong

I

At the throat of this tree he sees me kneel,
steep into leaves and pockets of shale.
My voice hollows out veins in roots:

I look to you to see you: fallen mouth from the sky.
Up where lips round off over descant—
steep into leaves and pockets of shale.

Open: rain-beaded blossom. Uvular angles.
Where rocks fall out of themselves, utter
up where lips round off over descant.

I want to go back to ruth, mouth ever so filled
to the lips before the fall. Word-spill,
where rocks fall out of themselves: utter

a prayer. Both limb and leaf bent skyward,
the calm before collapse. Creek-cut
at the lips before the fall. *A word-spill*

from leaf tongue, Father. From cracks,
the calm before collapse. Creek-cut
in the throat of this tree. He sees me kneel,
my voice hollows out veins in roots.

II

Scoop to hollow the bend, calm
to bend calm. See my right palm—
I'm going to bend calm again. Rock wrens
of eventide begin to warble the easy ends:
cut. Into the air sweet water sprays; psalm

to the ever-pouring gaze. A trickle bomb
as *my sore ran in the night*. When to embalm
this bubble stone walk and finally ascend,
scoop the hollowed.

Where the arrow current quells the qualm:
pierced, we say nothing. I glance at my palm—
it's where we began and didn't go, didn't lend
our eyes toward the current: whittled to bend,
a sand-swollen end, a silent opening.

III

O Holy People, show me how I am human,
how I am soon to sliver. Stay please, for woman
or man's sake. Succor me from a telestial state,
where I long to be self-luminous in a slate
of granite. How easily I fall to shards, a hand

left to wane ungathered. How easily we
gather rocks for pockets. What drowns
is not the boulder but swivel water bait,
O Diyin Diné'é!

Hook me by the ribs, bear me up to human,
so I know to come here only when it's a male
rain. This is how I dry my hair, kept from weight
of water. If all you can tell me is—*wait*,
let it be enough to know how sparkling can—
O Holy People.

Notes

Ach'íí'

Ach'íí' is a Navajo delicacy consisting of sheep intestines wrapped around dried stomach fat, then roasted over a fire.

Uranium mining on the Navajo Nation caused a number of unspeakable health defects to people (usually causing death) and land, from exposure to radiation and heavy metal contamination in soil and water.

The Indian Student Placement Program was part of the Church of Jesus Christ of Latter-day Saints from the 1940s to the early 1990s. After Native American children were baptized, they were given the opportunity to live with Latter-day Saint families in Utah, California, Idaho, and other states during the school year, to receive a better education and develop leadership while developing understandings between native and non-native peoples.

Sunbeam

To Navajos, seeing an owl is a bad omen, usually meaning death is coming.

"Jesus Wants Me for A Sunbeam" is a children's hymn with words written by Nellie Talbot and music by Edwin O. Excell.

Rising Song, Elegy

"Shádí" is the Navajo word for "my older sister."

The Church of Jesus Christ of Latter-day Saints teaches of baptism for the dead, but that children who die under the age of eight need not be baptized, as they are alive in Christ.

Calico Prints
See notes for "Ach'íí'."

Elegy for Yucca Fruit Woman
Navajo creation tells of a time when the people were once in dire
need of help. A large bird came to their rescue, taking them to safety,
and landing in what is modern-day Shiprock, New Mexico. Shiprock,
also know as Tsé Bit'a'í or "Rock With Wings," is believed to be that
bird who helped the people.

Nightsong
After a person passes on, especially after a sudden or unexpected
death, some Native American tribes light fires at home for the
departed spirits, so they will know where to go. The fire can stay lit for
three to five days, and at least one person is present, never leaving the
fire alone.

According to local tribes in New York, people who experience sudden
deaths have their spirits jarred and continue to dwell where they
died. They then become lonely, calling for others to come to them.
By offering food or songs to the spirit at the places where the deaths
occurred, those spirits can know they are not forgotten and will no
longer call for others to join them.

Navajos believe only the dead are dressed with rings on their thumbs
and forefingers. It's a way to tell if someone who comes to you is
dead.

To Gorge
Navajos tell of a time in history when there was a separation of the
sexes. First Man and First Woman had an argument that led them to
separate men from women and live for an extended amount of time
on different sides of a river. As they grew lonely, self-abuse became
prevalent by both men and women.

At Evil Canyon
Old Navajo masks once used for Ye'ii Bicheii ceremonies are hidden in
this canyon.

Leaping Ridge

Navajos tell of a massacre atop a ridge in Cove, Arizona, in the early 1800s. They fled from Mexican soldiers and withstood them for a time. Some lowered down people in the crevices of cliffs to escape.

Chokecherry Canyon

In a canyon just outside the Navajo border town of Farmington, New Mexico, three Navajo men were mutilated, bludgeoned, and burned to death in April 1974 by three white Farmington High School students.

"O the depravity of my people!" is taken from Moroni 9:18 in the *Book of Mormon*.

Flint Boys, Sky Map

In Western culture, Flint Boys is known as Pleaides.

Hand trembling is a type of Navajo divination used to identify and locate illnesses or lost items, animals, etc.

Evensong

The italicized line in Part II is taken from Psalms 77:2: "In the day of my trouble I sought the Lord: my sore ran in the night, and ceased not: my soul refused to be comforted."

In Part III, "The Holy People" translates into Navajo as "Diyin Diné'é."

According to LDS belief, the Telestial Kingdom is the lowest of the three degrees or kingdoms of glory in heaven. The scriptures compare the glory of the telestial kingdom to the glory of the stars.

Acknowledgments

Ahéhee' to my God for my passion and love of language, and for the power of language.

Thank you to Scott Nicolay for encouraging me greatly with my writing early on. To all my mentors and teachers, for your time and patience and kindness and support, thank you: Jon Davis, Evelina Lucero, Arthur Sze, Jane Hafen, Jim Barnes, Scott Hatch, Jolene Rickard, LyRae Van Clief-Stefanon, and Robert Morgan. To Alice Fulton, thank you for your sincerity and candor not only in poetry but also in life. And to Kenneth McClane, I will always be grateful not only for your enthusiasm and energy for this work but also for your respectful approach and continued support.

To the creative writing programs at the Institute of American Indian Arts and Cornell University, I give my sincerest thanks for the blessing it was to live and work in Santa Fe and Ithaca. To my BFA and MFA cohorts and workshop buddies, thank you for your work and friendships. And to my dear friends Layli Long Soldier and Benjamin Garcia, for your keen eyes and hearts invested in my work—to the both of you, I offer gracious thanks.

And finally to my dad and siblings, for your sharing of life, stories, and strength, ahéhee'.

CPSIA information can be obtained
at www.ICGtesting.com
Printed in the USA
LVHW032252211221
706846LV00006B/847